THE SPELLING BEE TOOLBOX™

FOR GRADES 3-5

*All the resources you need
for a successful Spelling Bee!*

by Ann Richmond Fisher

Cover image and design by Bryce A. Fisher

ISBN-13: 978-0692568705

ISBN-10: 0692568700

THE SPELLING BEE TOOLBOX ™
Table of Contents

THE SPELLING BEE TOOLBOX ™

Introduction

Dictionary.com defines a Spelling Bee as "a spelling competition won by the individual or team spelling the greatest number of words correctly." Of course, that's true, but a spelling bee is so much more!

A spelling bee motivates students to study spelling words. A spelling bee fosters healthy competition. It recognizes excellence in learning. It brings students into a well-defined structure and requires that they follow rules. And, a spelling bee is FUN!

Spelling bees are growing in popularity worldwide, as shown by the emails, comments and questions I've received from parents, teachers and students around the globe. Folks have requested even more tools than already appear on the website, and they've given me ideas for expanding the ones that are there.

As a result, in this book I've brought together the best tools from the website, all in one place, and I've expanded many of them. Plus, I've added those additional tools that site visitors have requested. You'll find more words, more sentences, more award certificates, more tips for teachers, and so much MORE of everything.

This is the second edition of the Spelling Bee Toolbox, revised and expanded, again based on feedback by website visitors and satisfied customers from around the globe. I've added more helpful resources including the FAQs, personnel chart, audience guidelines, additional certificates, games, worksheets, name tags, words/sentences and Super Challenge words. In all, I've added more than 20 extra pages.

This Spelling Bee Toolbox is truly the one resource you need for your own successful spelling bees!

Thanks for your support of www.spelling-words-well.com. Please keep the comments coming.

Ann
ann@spelling-words-well.com

THE SPELLING BEE TOOLBOX ™
Instructions

Students in elementary grades may have never before participated in a spelling bee, so make sure you give them a positive first experience! Read through all the instructions and choose the resources that best fit your students. In order to gain the maximum benefit from the tools in this eBook, please refer to the instructions for each section.

Guidelines for Three Kinds of Spelling Bees

The set of rules you choose to follow will depend on:

- The setting of your spelling bee
- The number of spellers who are participating
- The number of people involved in conducting the bee
- The time that's available for the bee

I recommend you read through the guidelines for all the types of bees listed here, and then pick and choose the features that will work best for your situation. (Please note the spelling games on page 22 which are good introductory activities for young spellers.) Once you've decided on the rules you'll use, be certain to make the rules clear to all the students, parents and teachers who will be involved in the activity. Then be sure to follow the rules consistently during the contest.

Organizing a Spelling Bee

Use this checklist to get organized and stay organized. Adjust the list as needed for your situation. If you are responsible for a large bee, please don't ignore this tool!

Personnel Chart

Here's a place to record everyone's name and phone number who is involved in your big bee. You may not need to fill every position, and you may need to add some that are not listed. Once you've filled out this page, make copies for others as needed.

Recorder's Chart

The recorder (or one of the judges) can use this helpful tool to keep track of which spellers are in and out of the competition. It's important to note the round on which each one is eliminated, the misspelled word, and the misspelling in case of disputes later. The first page is numbered for the first twenty students in the first 8 rounds. The second page can be photocopied as needed for subsequent rounds and additional spellers.

Audience Guidelines
Include some or all of these in your printed programs, or ask your emcee to read them at the beginning of any major spelling bee. Don't let unnecessary distractions upset your spellers! Be sure to cover #4 with your judges. Use it only with their agreement.

Family Letter
Use this letter as is, or adapt for your situation. It's essential to communicate early and often with families. You can also adapt this for email and Facebook posts.

Press Release
Members of the press won't know about your event unless you tell them! Use this format to formally announce your Bee to local newspapers, radio and television stations. Be sure to include the *who, what, where, when* info at the very beginning of your press release. Reporters love a good local story, so be sure to include interesting details about your bee that will draw their attention and make them *want* to promote your event!

Classroom Activities and Spelling Bee Games
Use these ideas to help students gain confidence in spelling in front of others and to increase their spelling proficiency. These ideas can be used year-round, even when your students are *not* participating in a spelling bee.

The Scripps Spelling Bee
This information answers some basic questions about the world's most famous bee. Use the links to learn more.

How to Study for a Spelling Bee
Give students this helpful guide as early as possible. Review the suggestions frequently in class.

Spelling Rules for Elementary Grades
This list includes a lot of the spelling rules that that students in grades 3-5 already know and a few more they should master before any spelling bee. Mastering these rules can give students clues about spelling words that are new to them in spelling bees.

Study List
These 100 words are a good sampling of words students might expect to encounter in any spelling bee. Approximately 70 of these words appear in the mega-list of 620 words in this eBook.

Worksheets
Use these formats to make more of your own worksheets using new words. You can even ask your *students* to help create worksheets to share with classmates. The more times students use their spelling words, the more likely they are to remember them.

Frequently Asked Questions

This brief sections covers some key points about the big word lists and study lists for students that I'm often asked. It's definitely worth a few minutes to read this page.

Spelling Bee Words and Sentences

Our list of 620 words was gleaned from a variety of grade-level resources. Many of the words appear in the spelling bee word lists on our website. Be sure to read through the words in advance of any spelling bee to rearrange, add and omit words as you see fit.

Also read through all the sentences prior to your competition. **Feel free to use your own sentences for any of the ones here that you feel are not meaningful or appropriate for your students.** Sentences are purposely brief. Many sentences give clues to the words' meanings as an aid to the speller. You don't need to use every word on the list. Skip over any words that you think might cause problems.

In general, our words appear from easiest to most difficult. However, this will not always be true for every speller. There are a few 2nd grade words included near the beginning of the list. As noted in the FAQ. If the words at the beginning of the list seem too easy for your group, you may skip them. You will still have plenty of words and sentences. There are many words at the 6th and 7th grade levels and beyond toward the end of the list.

You may start with any word on the list, depending on the level of your students. Here are some general guidelines:
Grade 3 – Start at the beginning
Grade 4 – Start around #150
Grade 5 – Start around #300

During the bee, you may choose to skip large sections of the list in order to get to more difficult words more quickly.

Alphabetical Listing of 620 Spelling Bee Words

This quick reference tool will allow you to compare our word list to your own spelling curriculum and other resources.

Super Challenge List

Use these words to challenge your best spellers or to supplement our list of 620 words during your spelling bee. Throughout the school year, be on the lookout for more super-challenge words to add to this list.

Clip art

Use these images to spruce up your flyers and letters. Here's one way to use our clip art as digital images:

1. Scroll to the page(s) with the image(s) you wish to use.
2. Press the "print screen" button on your keyboard.
3. Open up a new document in "Paint" or other image-editing program of your choice.
4. Insert the image from "print screen" by using Ctl + V or "insert"
5. Crop the image(s) you want. Resize as necessary.
6. In the file menu, click on "Save as." Name the file, save as a .jpg or .png in your documents or picture files in a location you can find later.
7. Open up a word document, then Insert --> Picture --> from file. Go to the saved location of your clip art image.
8. Adjust the image size as necessary as well as its layout properties. Complete your letter, announcement or other document.

Bookmarks

Photocopy these designs on card stock, cut apart and laminate.

Reminders

Use these for students, their families, and even spelling bee officials.

Name Tags

Photocopy enough to have one per student . Write in students' names and grade or other ID information and laminate, if desired. Cut out. Punch holes in upper corners and add string or yarn so that name tags can be hung around students' necks, as shown.

Award Certificates

Choose the awards that best fit the mood of your competition – serious, fun, modern, or traditional – in either color or black and white. You can follow either of these procedures in presenting the awards:

1) Print out the certificates of your choice prior to your spelling bee. After the bee, write in the winners' names and present them immediately or at a later date.
2) After the bee, open the certificates of your choice in a pdf-editing program. Insert the winners' names and print. Present the awards at a later ceremony

THE SPELLING BEE TOOLBOX ™
Classroom Spelldown

This is a great format to use in your classroom in a single class period. The "team spirit" factor helps spellers encourage one another. Misspelled words are spelled again and again until they're corrected, making this a valuable instructional tool. (For more classroom spelling games that are great for elementary students, please see page 22.)

1. Divide students into two teams.

2. Each team lines up on opposite sides of the room, facing each other.

3. The teacher reads the first word to Player 1 on Team A. She also uses the word in a sentence.

4. Player 1 repeats the word, spells it, and says the word again.

5. If the player is correct, he moves to the end of the line on team A. The teacher gives the next word to the first player on Team B. If the player is incorrect, the player sits down and is out of the spelldown. The teacher gives the same word to player 1 on Team B.

6. Player 1 on Team B repeats the word, spells it, and says the word again.

7. If she is correct, she moves to the end of the line on her team.

8. The Spelldown continues with correct players moving to the end of the line, and incorrect players leaving the competition. Eventually, the students who have spelled correctly will move to the front of the line to spell again and again. At some point, one team will have only one speller. That student must spell every time it's his team's turn.

9. The spelldown ends when one team has lost all its spellers. The winning team is the one with the last speller(s) standing.

Variation:
If the same word is misspelled by two (or choose a different number) players, both players *remain in the spelldown*. The teacher writes the correct spelling of the missed word on the board and gives those players a new word to spell.

THE SPELLING BEE TOOLBOX ™
Classroom Spelling Bee

This individual competition is slightly more competitive than the spelldown, but not as rigid as the formal spelling bee, outlined below.

1. Determine the order in which students will spell. Arrange spellers in that order in their seats or in an open area of the classroom.

2. The teacher announces the word to be spelled. He speaks slowly and clearly, without distorting the normal pronunciation of the word. He uses the word in a sentence and says the word again.

3. The speller listens carefully to the teacher and asks for the word to be repeated if necessary.

4. When the speller is sure she understands the word, she pronounces it, spells it and then says the word again.

5. The teacher determines whether or not the word was spelled correctly.

6. If the correct spelling was given, the speller remains in the bee.

7. If the spelling was incorrect, that speller is eliminated from the bee. The teacher gives the correct spelling of that word. Then the teacher reads a new word to the next student.

8. The bee continues until all but two spellers have been eliminated. When there are only two spellers left, if one player misspells a word, the other player must spell that word correctly, plus one more word to be declared the winner of the spelling bee.

THE SPELLING BEE TOOLBOX ™
All-School (or Large) Spelling Bee

For this type of spelling bee, you'll need several officials: a pronouncer, at least one judge, a recorder and, optionally, a timekeeper. See list on page 16.

The spelling bee coordinator should select officials for these positions who speak clearly, listen carefully and who will follow the guidelines you present to them.

Advance preparation needed by the spelling bee officials:

Judges
Read the rules and the word list. Select and secure a large dictionary to use on the day of the bee. Designate one person as the head judge who will make the final decisions on the correct or incorrect spelling of a word.

Pronouncer
Read through the word list in advance. Look up the correct pronunciation of any unfamiliar words in the designated dictionary. Learn the rules for the bee.

Recorder
Read the rules and word list in advance. Review the recorder's chart.

Timekeeper-Optional (See rule 4B)
During the bee, the timekeeper uses a stopwatch to keep track of the amount of time the speller uses to complete the spelling of each word. The time limit must be decided in advance and announced to all participants. A limit of 30 - 40 seconds is recommended, depending on the age of the students, the difficulty of the words, and the available time for the bee.

Spelling bee coordinator
Be sure to meet with the spelling bee officials prior to the bee to make sure all the rules and procedures are clear.

Immediately before the bee begins:

(For a more complete checklist, see page 13.)

1. Decide the order in which the students will participate. Seat them in order on stage, or at the front of the room.

2. Arrange a table for the judges and recorder.

3. Be sure all members of the audience are seated and quiet.

To conduct the bee, the head judge reads the rules and procedures aloud to the spellers and audience. He asks the spellers if they have any questions about the rules.

Rules:

1. The first speller goes to the microphone.

2. The pronouncer announces the word to be spelled. He speaks slowly and clearly, without distorting the normal pronunciation of the word. He uses the word in a sentence and says the word again.

3. The speller listens carefully to the pronouncer and asks for the word to be repeated if necessary.

4. When the speller is sure she understands the word, she pronounces it, spells it and then says the word again. She must say it loudly enough for the judge(s) to hear it.

Optional additions to this rule:
    A. Once a speller has started spelling the word, she may start over as long as she has not finished spelling the word and repeated it.   **OR**
    Once a speller has started to spell the word, she may not start over.

    B. Spellers will have a time limit of ___ seconds in which to complete the spelling of the word, from the time she indicates to the pronouncer that she understands the word she is to spell.

5. The judge(s) determines whether or not the word was spelled correctly.

6. If the correct spelling was given, the speller remains in the bee and goes back to her seat.

7. If the spelling was incorrect, that speller is eliminated from bee. The speller leaves the stage at the end of the round, i.e. after each speller has taken one turn. (Optional variations: The speller leaves the stage immediately.)

8. If the word was misspelled, the judge gives the correct spelling of that word. Then the pronouncer reads a new word to the next student.

9. This process continues with correct spellers staying in the competition and incorrect spellers being eliminated. **Exception:** If *all* remaining spellers are eliminated in the same round, then all spellers should be brought back into the competition.

10. When there are only two spellers left, if one player misspells a word, the other player must spell that word correctly, plus one more word, to be declared the winner of the spelling bee.

THE SPELLING BEE TOOLBOX ™
Organizational Checklist

Use this checklist to plan a school-wide or district-wide spelling bee. Check off each task as it is completed.

6-12 months in advance

- ☐ Form a group of 3-4 people to help organize the spelling bee.

- ☐ Decide what schools, grades or ages will compete in your spelling bee.

- ☐ Set the date.

- ☐ Reserve the facilities you will need.

- ☐ Notify teachers, students, parents, and administrators of the date of the bee and the eligibility requirements.

- ☐ Discuss the funds that will be needed for the event. Learn what resources are already available and how much more money you may need to raise.

- ☐ Contact local businesses, if necessary, to help fund your event.

3-6 months in advance

- ☐ Decide what word lists you will use. Let spellers know in advance. We recommend the list of 620 words in this book. But you may decide to make your own list based on your own spelling curriculum. The Scripps National Spelling Bee uses *Webster's Third New International Dictionary* and its Addenda Section (copyright 2002 by Merriam-Webster), which means those spellers must be ready for anything! Whatever you decide, be sure that students have at least some of the words in advance and/or know what dictionary you'll be using.

- ☐ Choose your Spelling Bee pronouncer, judges, record keeper, and timekeeper, if needed. Double-check their availability for your date.

- ☐ Double-check on the availability of your facility.

- ☐ If your bee will be held at a location other than your own school, arrange to have someone attend your event that is familiar with the building. Be sure you have someone to run the sound system.

- ☐ Decide on the spelling bee rules you will use. (See page 11 for our suggestions.) Send written copies to students, parents, teachers, and all bee officials.

- ☐ Decide if you want to serve refreshments and if so, what type of foods and beverages you want to include. Then find a very responsible person to be in charge of that portion of the event.

1-2 months in advance

- ❑ Decide on prizes. Choose award certificates included in this book, or order medals and trophies from local vendors or online sources. (Allow at least 6 weeks for special orders.)

- ❑ Check back with all participants frequently. One month before the spelling bee, send a note to all classrooms and bee officials reminding them of the date. Tell them what time they should arrive at the competition.

- ❑ Get a list of the names of all students who expect to participate.

- ❑ Notify local newspapers, radio stations, and TV stations to let them know about the spelling bee. See the Sample Press Release on page 20.

- ❑ Invite sponsors to attend.

1-2 weeks in advance

- ❑ Announce the bee on your Face Book page and other social media.

- ❑ If you're using a stage, be sure you have chairs, a podium, microphones, and tables for the judges.

- ❑ Make name tags for all participants and officials.

- ❑ Print out word lists for the pronouncers and judges. Print the recorder's chart (pages 16-17) for the record keeper. Gather dictionaries, pencils, and a stopwatch.

- ❑ Contact media personnel again and encourage them to cover your big event.

The day of the Spelling Bee

- ❑ Arrive 2 hours early with your word lists, dictionaries, recorder's charts, pencils, awards and name tags.

- ❑ Check the sound system and seating.

- ❑ Welcome your spellers, staff and audience.

- ❑ Publicly thank sponsors, spellers, teachers, parents, staff and media.

- ❑ *Enjoy the bee!*

After the Spelling Bee

- ❑ Clean up the facility, if necessary.

- ❑ Announce the spelling bee winners in public forums.

- ❑ Send a thank you note to everyone who helped with the bee.

- ❑ Recover and start planning for next year!

THE SPELLING BEE TOOLBOX ™
Personnel

	Name	Phone number/Email address
Coordinator	_____	_____
Central Planning Team	_____	_____
	_____	_____
	_____	_____
	_____	_____
Emcee	_____	_____
Judge (s)	_____	_____
	_____	_____
Pronouncer	_____	_____
Recorder	_____	_____
Timekeeper	_____	_____
Sound technician	_____	_____
Facilities manager	_____	_____
Publicity coordinator	_____	_____
_____	_____	_____
_____	_____	_____
_____	_____	_____
_____	_____	_____

THE SPELLING BEE TOOLBOX ™
Recorder's Chart

Student	Round								Misspelled Word
	1	2	3	4	5	6	7	8	
Example: Jane Doe	✓	✓	✓	✓	X				acter
1.									
2.									
3.									
4.									
5.									
6.									
7.									
8.									
9.									
10.									
11.									
12.									
13.									
14.									
15.									
16.									
17.									
18.									
19.									
20.									

THE SPELLING BEE TOOLBOX ™
Recorder's Chart – Additional pages

Student	Round								Misspelled Word

THE SPELLING BEE TOOLBOX ™
Audience Guidelines

Thank you for attending our spelling bee. Your support means so much to our spellers! In order to help them concentrate and perform at their very best, please observe these guidelines:

1. During each round, remain quiet and in your seat.

2. If you must leave your seat, please wait until the end of a round to leave the room. Also wait until the end of a round to reenter the room.

3. Do not spell any word aloud. Do not even whisper it to yourself or to your neighbor.

4. Do not argue with the judges. Their decisions are final. If you feel strongly that a mistake was made, please write down what you observed.

At the end of that round, ask the judges for a moment of their time. It is their option to receive your comment or not, and to act upon it, or not. Again, their decisions are final.

5. Hold your applause until the end of the spelling bee, as instructed by the spelling bee officials.

Spelling Bee News!

Dear Families,

A very important event involving your student is coming up! Please mark this information on your calendar now.

The _____ Spelling Bee

Date:

Time:

Location:

Here are several ways you can help your student prepare for the Bee:

1) Help your student study spelling words frequently. Ask him/her to spell them aloud. You can study word lists that I will be sending home, words from other textbooks, words from the newspaper and unfamiliar words from the dictionary.

2) On the week of the Spelling Bee, and especially the night before the Bee, make sure your student gets plenty of rest and proper nutrition.

3) If at all possible, plan to attend the Bee. If you are unable to attend, please try to arrange for another family member or friend to be there. Your presence will be a huge encouragement to *all* of our students.

If I can be of further assistance, please contact me at:_____

Thank you in advance for your support!

Sincerely,

Sample Press Release

Fisher Elementary School
123 Scholarly Drive
Lansing, MI 49ZIP
(123) 456-7890

FOR IMMEDIATE RELEASE   **Contact:** John Doe, Spelling Bee Coordinator
(123) 456-7890 x987

10th Annual Fisher Elementary School Spelling Bee – November 9

Lansing, MI – On Tuesday, November 9, at 10 A.M, the Fisher Elementary School will hold its tenth annual spelling bee competition in the school's auditorium. Admission is free and open to the public.

Twenty-four students from grades 3, 4, and 5 will compete for the title of school champion. The champion will represent the school next month in the Ingham County Spelling Bee.

Mayor Sue Jones will be on hand to present the trophy to this year's winner. The winner will also receive a $100 U.S. Savings Bond, compliments of Acme Services, this year's sponsor.

School principal, Ms. Sondra Smith, notes that two past winners of Fisher Elementary School Spelling Bee have gone on to compete at the state and national levels. She urges the public to attend the event and encourage the hard-working students.

Each participant has already competed at his/her own grade level and finished among the top 8 in his/her class. During the all-school competition, participants will be asked to spell words from lists they have not previewed. It should prove to be a challenging competition for all students.

For more information about the Fisher Elementary School Spelling Bee, please contact *John Doe at 123.456.7890.987 or j.doe@email.address.*

THE SPELLING BEE TOOLBOX ™
Classroom Activities

You can help your students prepare for spelling bees all year long. Their success in spelling bees will depend on two factors:
A) Spelling proficiency
B) Confidence spelling aloud in front of others

To help students gain proficiency in their spelling skills:

1) Challenge students each week with a few tough words. Write the words on the board at the beginning of each week and discuss their meanings. Include these difficult words on the weekly spelling quiz and in other written assignments. Use words from their other subjects, such as science, social students, and math. Also refer to the list of spelling bee words at the end of this book, word lists at www.spelling-words-well.com and/or the dictionary.

2) Ask students to contribute the challenge words. Assign a different pair of students each week to find 5 difficult words. At the beginning of each week, the two students can do a brief oral presentation in which they write the words on the board and explain their meanings.

3) Review common spelling rules with students. See pages 27-28.

4) Give students extra written practice with difficult words. Reading and writing are essential experiences, especially for visual learners.

5) Frequently review commonly misspelled words such as *enough, friend,* and *neighbor.*

To help students gain confidence in spelling aloud:

1) Conduct frequent, brief oral quizzes. At the beginning or end of a class period, use just a minute or two for "popcorn" quizzes. Randomly call out a student's name and a spelling word. For example, say "Rachel, *always.*" Rachel pops up and spells always. If she's incorrect, call on the student seated behind her, "Ali, *always.*," and so on. This not only gives frequent practice, it motivates students to study the weekly spelling words.

2) Ask students to do oral reading, oral math, or any kind of oral presentation from their seats and especially in front of the class.

3) Play our spelling bee games on pages 22-23.

THE SPELLING BEE TOOLBOX ™
Spelling Bee Games

Here are four simple, fun games to help get your students ready for a spelling bee. The only supplies you'll need are the chalkboard and chalk (or whiteboards and markers). You can play these games anytime throughout the year, with any list of spelling words.

Spelling Relay

1. Divide your class into two teams. Each team forms a single line.

2. Divide the board into two sections, one for each team.

3. To play, the first player from each team comes to the board. The teacher calls out a spelling word, and each player writes the first letter of the word.

4. The first player races back to the line and hands the chalk/marker to the next player. The next player adds the second letter returns to the line and hands off the marker, the third player adds the third letter, and so on.

5. The first team to finish the word correctly earns one point.

Note: If a player makes a mistake, instead of adding a new letter, the next teammate corrects the mistake. He does not add a new letter. Players will see that this slows down the completion of the word, so they'll want to try hard to get the right letters the first time.

Team Spelling

1. Ask students to "count off" into four groups. Then seat all the 1s together, all the 2s together, and so on.

2. Divide the board into 4 sections and number them, so that each team has one section of the board on which to write.

3. To play, ask the first person on each team to come to the board. Pronounce the first spelling word. The first person to finish the word correctly wins a point for his team.

4. For the next spelling word, the second person from each team comes to the board.

5. At the end of playing time, the team with the most points is the winner.

Tic Tac Toe Spelling Game

Here's another super-simple spelling game that you can play with the whole class, or in small groups, in a short or long period of class time. You may ask students to spell words orally or to write them on the board.

1. Draw a tic-tac-toe game on the board.

2. Divide students into two groups. Assign one team to be the Xs, and one team to be the O's.

3. To play, one member from each team goes to the board. Pronounce a spelling word for the X team.

4. If the X player **correctly** spells the word, he may put an X on the tic-tac-toe game. If he spells the word **incorrectly**, he may not put an X on the game. A new member of his team goes to the board to wait for her turn.

5. Then pronounce a new word for the O team and proceed in the same manner.

6. The first team to get three Xs or three O's in a row wins the round.

Buzz-Buzz Spelling Word Game

In this fast-paced game, students spell words orally, one letter per person.

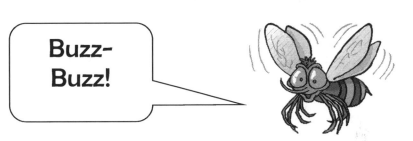

Buzz-Buzz!

1. Divide the class into two teams.

2. Call out the first word to Team 1. The first player orally gives the first letter, the second player states the second letter, etc.

3. When the last letter has been given, the next player says, "Buzz-Buzz, we're right," or "Oh no, we're wrong!"
   - If the word was spelled correctly, and the final player correctly stated it was correct, then whoever started that word sits down.
   - If the last player gave the wrong assessment of the team's spelling, then he sits down.
   - If the word was spelled incorrectly, the person who gave the wrong letter sits down.

4. Play until there are only two players left on each team. Then ask everyone to rejoin their teams and play again, as time allows.

The Scripps Spelling Bee

No spelling bee resource would be complete without mentioning the Scripps Spelling Bee, the oldest national spelling competition in the United States. It began in 1925 and is run as a not-for-profit competition by the E.W. Scripps Company. It is the "bee of all spelling bees" with final rounds aired on television stations around the world.

Eligibility

In order to be eligible to compete in the Scripps National Spelling Bee, students must attend a school that is enrolled in the Scripps program. (See Scripps FAQs for rules regarding homeschooled students.) Students must be under the age of 16 and in grades 8 or below. Schools must enroll with the national office from mid-August through mid-October and pay a fee to participate.

Participating schools are located in the U.S., Canada, Puerto Rico, New Zealand, South Korea, U.S. Department of Defense schools in Europe, and several other locations.

The Process

While different regions follow different plans, usually schools hold several small competitions. For example, each classroom might hold its own bee. Then the winners from each classroom might compete against each other in school wide spelling bee. Next, the winners from several schools in the same city or county might compete against each other. Regional and statewide competitions may also follow.

Normally, champions compete at several levels before moving on to the finals which are held at the Grand Hyatt Hotel in Washington, D.C. The finals are always held during the week following Memorial Day.

Preparation

Students who are serious about competing in Scripps study all year long, for hours every day. Students in enrolled schools can receive lists of words to study from Scripps. Merriam-Webster also provides study helps. In addition to learning the spellings of words, it is also very helpful students to learn definitions, pronunciations, parts of speech and etymologies of words.

Many champion students study straight from the *Third New International Dictionary of the English Language,* the official dictionary used by Scripps. They also read good books to learn new words. Students often keep a special list of their own interesting words to memorize.

Prizes

The champion of the annual Scripps National Spelling Bee receives a generous prize package including a large amount of cash, a huge trophy, and reference books. All spellers who make it to the finals receive prizes, based on the number of rounds they successfully complete.

Helpful links:

Home page for the Scripps Spelling Bee: http://www.spellingbee.com/
Complete student eligibility rules: http://www.spellingbee.com/eligibility
FAQs for Scripps: http://www.spellingbee.com/customer-service-center
Past champions: http://www.spellingbee.com/champions-and-their-winning-words

THE SPELLING BEE TOOLBOX ™
How to Study for a Spelling Bee

In a weekly spelling quiz, you know exactly which words you'll be asked to spell. But in a spelling bee, you could be asked to spell just about anything! So what's the best way to prepare to spell well at your next competition?

There are several strategies you should use. Some are long-term practices, and others can be used at the last minute to boost your skills.

Long term - What you should do all year long

1. Keep a spelling notebook. Write down words that are tricky for you, including words you've misspelled on spelling quizzes or writing assignments. Also write down words that you don't know how to spell very well. Read over the words in your notebook frequently.

2. Read a lot to expand to learn new words. As you read, you'll learn new words and how to use them. Add the most interesting words and the ones with the trickiest spellings to your notebook.

3. Be sure to learn the spelling words you're given in class each week, as well as vocabulary words from science, social studies and math classes.

4. Practice difficult words over and over. Write them on paper, and type them into a text document on the computer. Ask someone to quiz you aloud on the words. All of this practice helps you to remember the words when you're in a spelling bee.

5. Try different ways to spell words when you're on stage. At home, practice spelling words aloud, using one of these methods:
- Trace it in the air or on the back of your hand with your finger
- Say it to yourself
- Picture it in your mind

Which way works the best for you? Once you figure it out, use it once or twice a week as you spell words aloud with a friend or family member. Get comfortable with spelling tricky words in front of other people.

6. Learn basic spelling strategies and rules. (See page 27-28.) In your notebook, make a list of commonly-used words that are exceptions to these rules.

7. If you're really serious about advancing to regional, state or national competitions, you need to get a good dictionary and study it. Many older students use *Webster's New International Dictionary of the English Language, Unabridged*, the largest dictionary of the English language. It's the one used by the Scripps' National Spelling Bee, making it the perfect one to study for advanced spelling bee competitions.

8. Talk to other students who have done well in spelling bees. Talk to older students, your brothers or sisters, or classmates who have done well. What tips worked for them? You can also read books about successful spellers, including *How to Spell Like a Champ* by Trinkle, Andrews and Kimble.

Short term - What you can do weeks or days before the spelling bee

1. Ask your teacher for specific list of words you can study. See the word lists at www.spelling-words-well.com if you need more words. Then study!

2. Review all the words in your spelling book, especially those that were hard to learn.

3. Practice spelling a lot of words aloud with a friend or family member. Ask a parent or older sibling to quiz you while you're riding in the car, walking to the store, or anytime.

4. Post spelling words everywhere: the bathroom mirror, the computer desktop, your school desk or locker. Carry a list of words you want to learn in your pocket. Pull out the list and study it when you have spare minutes between other activities.

5. Review homonyms such as *rain/rein/reign, capital/capitol,* and *cymbal/symbol.* Be sure you know the correct usage of each word.

6. Ask someone to quiz you on words that you haven't studied before. They can find these words in a library book or on the front page of a newspaper.

7. Review the tips in the long-term list above and work on them as much as possible.

8. The night before the spelling bee, get plenty of rest. Eat a good breakfast in the morning. Include some protein, such as eggs, cheese or peanut butter.

9. Most importantly, believe you can do it! Your preparation will give you confidence to think clearly and spell correctly, even if you feel a little bit nervous!

THE SPELLING BEE TOOLBOX ™
Spelling Rules for Elementary Grades

Go over the spelling rules you've already learned before any competition. Also review words that are exceptions to the rules. These rules may help you figure out how to spell new words in a spelling bee. Here are 14 rules and exceptions to review.

1. Compound Words
Keep both words whole. Don't drop the last letter of the first word or the first letter of the last word. Examples: roommate, bookkeeper, sidewalk, withhold.

2. Contractions
First make sure to spell the **correct** word. For example, listen to the sentence to know if you should spell *they're, their* or *there* and *who's* or *whose*. Then be sure to include the apostrophe in place of the missing letter.

3. Words spelled with *ie* or *ei*
Use *i* before *e* except after *c* or when sounded like *a* as in *neighbor* and *weigh*. Examples: friend, believe, ceiling, receive, eight, vein. There are many exceptions to this rule, including: *neither, science, their, weird,* and others. Memorize these.

<u>Forming Plurals</u>

4. Words that end in s,x,z, ch, or sh
To make these word plural, add es. Examples: boxes, churches, bushes, glasses.

5. Words that end in *y*
A) If a noun ends in a consonant followed by a *y,* change the *y* to *i* and add *es.* Examples: babies, stories

B) If a noun ends in a vowel followed by a *y,* add *s.* Examples: chimneys, turkeys

6. Words that end in *f or fe*
A) Most nouns ending in *f* or *fe* form the plural by changing the *f* or *fe* to *v* and adding -es. Examples: knife/knives, hoof/hooves, loaf/loaves
Exception: roof/roofs

B) For a double *f,* just add *s.* Examples: puff/puffs, cliff/cliffs.

loaves

7. Making plurals from words that end in *o*
A) If a vowel comes before the final o, add s. Examples: radios, studios

B) If a consonant comes before the final o, usually add es. Examples: potatoes, echoes
The plural forms of *mosquito* and *tornado* can be spelled either way.

Interesting note: The plural of most words related to music that end in o are formed by adding *s* only. Examples: solos, pianos

Adding Prefixes

8. When adding prefixes such as *dis- mis-, pre- re-, un,* the spelling of the base word does not change.
Examples: disable, misspell, redo, unusual.

Adding Suffixes

9. Doubling the final consonant
If a one-syllable word ends with a vowel followed by a consonant, double the consonant before adding the suffix. Examples: stopping, bedding, dipper

Note that words like *lead* become *leading* because there are two vowels before the final consonant. Words like *helping* have one *p* because they end in two consonants.

10. Words that end in *e*
A) Drop the *e* when the suffix begins with a vowel. (-ed, -ing, -ous, -able, –y)
Examples: closed, hoping, nervous, edgy. Exceptions: noticeable, courageous
A few words can be spelled either way: loveable or lovable, movable or moveable.

B) Keep the silent *e* when the suffix begins with a consonant (-ment, -ful, -ly)
Example: hopeful, movement.   Exceptions: ninth, truly

11. Adding *-less*
The base word does not usually change. Examples: hopeless, clueless.

12. Adding *-ful*
The suffix *–ful* never has two ls. When *–ful* is added to a word, the spelling of the base word usually does not change.
Examples: helpful, cheerful, careful.

13. Adding *–dom* and *–ship*
The base word does not usually change. Examples: friendship, freedom, kingdom.

14. The sound of /shun/
This sound is usually spelled –tion, and less often –sion. Examples: motion, nation, station, tension, mansion.

mansion

THE SPELLING BEE TOOLBOX ™
Study List for Students

Here are 100 words to learn before your next spelling bee.

1. absence
2. acre
3. active
4. actor
5. almost
6. answer
7. aunt
8. bakery
9. balcony
10. beautiful
11. bread
12. build
13. careful
14. castle
15. caught
16. champion
17. children
18. chimneys
19. clothes
20. coming
21. daughter
22. desert
23. dinner
24. discover
25. doesn't
26. eight
27. elect
28. embarrass
29. except
30. famous
31. February
32. freezer
33. gloomy
34. grown

35. guess
36. happiest
37. haven't
38. heavy
39. hopeful
40. ignore
41. I'll
42. interested
43. inventor
44. judge
45. juice
46. kitchen
47. knowledge
48. library
49. likely
50. listen
51. manager
52. mirror
53. moist
54. monkeys
55. necessary
56. nephew
57. noisy
58. observe
59. occur
60. opposite
61. order
62. paper
63. paragraph
64. people
65. piece
66. pleasure
67. probably
68. queen

69. question
70. radios
71. reach
72. received
73. sandwich
74. Saturday
75. science
76. secret
77. separate
78. shovel
79. someone
80. spread
81. straighten
82. supplying
83. syllable
84. taxi
85. television
86. temperature
87. thumb
88. tomorrow
89. Tuesday
90. uniform
91. useful
92. verse
93. video
94. weight
95. wheat
96. whole
97. written
98. yogurt
99. zipper
100. zone

desert

Take a Look!

How many words in the list can be found in the puzzle? Use these rules to find out.

1. You may start at any letter and move one space in any direction to another letter that is next to it.
2. Don't go back to the same space in any one word, but use the letters over and over for different words.
3. Some examples of words you can make are: SOW, WATER, and HURT.

Now look for the words in the puzzle. Write the ones you find in the blanks below the puzzle. You will not be able to find all of the words in the puzzle.

Word List:
ruin
straight
tenth
heard
quite
quiet
wrist
radios
tries
striped
said
interrupt
phase
toward
unite
theater
sore
drawer

U	I	S	O	E
N	R	W	T	R
R	T	E	A	D
I	U	H	S	I
Q	T	P	G	O

Write ALL of the words from the word list in ABC order:

_____

_____

_____

_____

_____

_____

_____

_____

_____

_____

_____

_____

_____

_____

_____

_____

_____

_____

_____

_____

_____

_____

Smelly Scents?

Choose the correct homonym in to complete each
sentence. Write the word in the blank.

scents/cents
1. If your coins fell into the garbage, you might have smelly
_____.

2. If you didn't like your mom's perfumes, you'd say she had smelly _____.

ants/aunts
3. If you like to eat chocolate covered insects, you'd say you're having _____
for dinner.

4. If your father's sisters are coming to visit, you'd say you're having your
_____ over for dinner.

dear/deer
5. If your grandma is very fond of you, she'd call you her _____ grandchild.

6. If she spotted an animal outside the window, she'd say, "Come look at the
_____, my grandchild!"

meat/meet
7. If you need to buy something to eat, you'd go out to buy some _____.

8. If you want to see a friend, you'd go out to _____ him.

their/there/they're
9. If you thought your friends left some games at your house, you'd ask if
_____ missing some games.

10. If they can't find the games, they might ask you if they left _____ games at
your house.

Whose/Who's
11. If you wonder why part of your lunch is missing, you might ask, "_____ been
eating my lunch?"

12. If you found someone else's lunch, you might ask, "_____ lunch is this?"

On the back of this page, write sentences for these homonym sets:
> nose/knows   wait/weight   rain/rein/reign

Threesomes

Fit each three-letter word into the blanks in the longer words below, one letter at a time to complete a common word. You should be able to match the words so that you use each three-letter word exactly once.

and	awe	cut	ice	lot	one	pie
rot	~~sad~~	see	tea	tie	wig	

Example: __ p r e __ __ + s a d = s p r e a d

1. a __ m __ s __

2. s __ __ __ a l

3. n __ __ k __ l

4. __ a __ g h __

5. __ e __ __ h t

6. __ __ s s u __

7. s __ r __ __ k

8. __ n __ e z __

9. l __ __ y __ r

10. p __ __ m p __

11. l __ __ __ l y

12. __ __ c k l __ __

Wise With Words

If a word in the box is spelled correctly, you can find it in the puzzle. Circle each one that you find and cross if off the list. Words may appear in any direction.

If the word is not spelled correctly in the word list, it is not in the puzzle. Write it correctly in one of the blanks.

For extra fun, try to find one correctly-spelled word that appears TWO times in the puzzle. What is it? _____

l	x	t	t	n	e	f	l	k	s	f	n	g
f	o	s	s	i	l	d	a	n	i	p	y	y
y	x	g	e	f	u	a	o	n	u	e	t	t
e	x	c	i	d	g	g	a	l	v	d	g	p
n	e	b	l	b	e	l	r	e	p	a	i	e
o	e	t	r	h	l	c	r	i	r	x	n	c
u	n	e	a	y	e	y	e	b	n	i	e	x
g	o	i	e	c	o	l	a	i	m	n	s	e
h	u	g	u	n	u	g	e	r	v	u	e	u
k	g	h	e	f	e	d	e	v	o	e	g	d
m	h	t	y	r	u	t	e	m	e	p	u	b
o	t	h	o	y	e	c	a	h	w	n	m	h
b	r	x	c	d	o	f	w	c	y	v	h	t

Word List:

deceive
delicous
determine
diferent
dinosore
doller
doutful
earliest
educate
eighth
eleven
enough
especialy
everyone
except
explode
famous
finally
forgoten
forteen
fossil
frieght
garbage
grinned

_____   _____

_____   _____

_____   _____

_____   _____

_____

Riddle Time

What's more amazing than a talking parrot?

Use the clues to unscramble each word.
Then write your answers in the diagram.

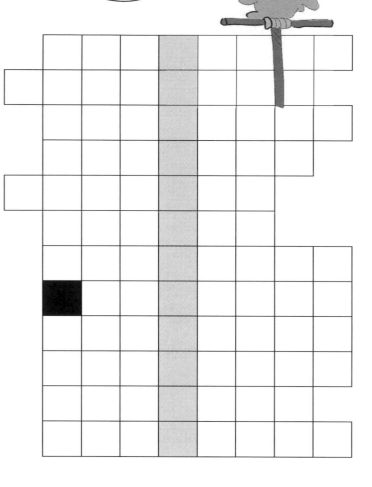

1. take apart: a p r s t a e e

2. totally different: s t o p i p e o

3. astonish: p r u s i r e s

4. positive: f o e p u h l

5. alike: a m i l i r s

6. actually: l y e r a l

7. certain: f i t e d i n e

8. at last: l a n i f y l

9. lives nearby: g r i n e b o h

10. likely: r a b b o p e l

11. accept: v e r i c e e

12: memorize: b r m e e r e m

Write the letters from the shaded squares, in order, in the blanks below to find the answer to the riddle.

What's more amazing than a talking parrot?

__ _____   _____ !

Directions, Please!

Follow the directions below the chart to reveal
a hidden message.

	A	B	C	D	E
1	Saturday	Doller	Straight	pennys	Nickel
2	Zebras	opossum	Turkys	Dinosuars	monkeys
3	Important	slippry	sneeze	library	stripes
4	carryed	have	stretch	trys	wiggle
5	potato	pumkin	pickel	zucchini	whistle

1. In Row 2, cross out each misspelled animal word.

2. In Row 5, cross out each misspelled food.

3. In Row 1, cross out each misspelled money word.

4. In Column E, circle each correctly spelled two-syllable word.

5. In Column C, circle each correctly spelled one-syllable word.

6. Cross out each misspelled word containing a Y remaining in the chart.

7. Underline each correctly spelled word of three syllables in the chart.

8. Write the unmarked words here, from left to right to spell a simple statement.

Under Construction

Use a base word with a suffix to spell a word that makes sense in each sentence. You will have to use some base words more than once.

Base words:
depend   disagree   Suffixes:
arrange   excite   able
believe   honor   ly
beautiful   immediate   ment
careful   measure

1. Carl's Construction Company gets a lot of work because Carl is honest and
_____.

2. Carl always makes a clear _____ with all of his clients about what he will do.

3. He gives _____ estimates and reasonable schedules of when the work will be finished.

4. Each day on the construction site, it's easy to see _____ progress being made.

5. Homeowners are filled with _____ when they see their home improvements taking shape.

6. There is seldom any _____ about whether the work is done properly.

7. If there is a complaint, Carl deals with the problem _____.

8. Carl trains his crew to work _____ to avoid injury and property damage.

9. They make careful _____ of all materials to avoid wasting supplies.

10. Carl tries not to hire crew members who are frequently _____.

11. Carl's customers say his remodeling jobs are done _____ and professionally.

12. He is an _____, hard-working business owner.

Answers to Worksheets

Take a Look

All words except *quiet, striped, tenth, tries* and *unite* are in the puzzle.

ABC order:
1. drawer
2. heard
3. interrupt
4. phase
5. quiet
6. quite
7. radios
8. ruin
9. said
10. sore
11. straight
12. striped
13. tenth
14. theater
15. toward
16. tries
17. unite
18. wrist

Smelly Scents?

1. cents 2. scents 3. ants 4. aunts 5. dear
6. deer 7. meat 8. meet 9. they're 10. their
11. Who's 12. Whose

Threesomes

1. almost	2. sandal	3. nickel	4. caught
5. weight	6. tissue	7. streak	8. sneeze
9. lawyer	10. prompt	11. lonely	12. pickle

Directions, Please

Zebras have stripes.

Riddle Time

A Spelling Bee!

Wise With Words

The word *enough* appears twice in the puzzle. Corrected spellings are: delicious, different, dinosaur, dollar, doubtful, especially, forgotten, fourteen, freight. (Also see puzzle diagram.)

Under Construction

1. dependable or honorable
2. arrangement
3. believable
4. measurable
5. excitement
6. disagreement
7. immediately
8. carefully
9. measurement
10. disagreeable
11. beautifully
12. honorable

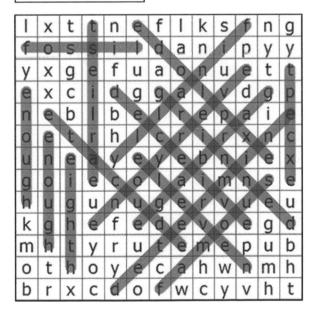

THE SPELLING BEE TOOLBOX ™

Frequently Asked Questions

Question: Why are there easy words at the beginning of the big list of words and sentences in the Toolbox?

Answer: There are easy words so that *all* of your students may enjoy participating in a spelling bee! The Toolbox is designed for general school and community use, with the idea that as many students as possible will want to be included. Many times, most students can succeed through at least the first round and feel successful.

As explained in the directions, please feel free to skip over any words that way too easy, or otherwise unsuitable for your purposes. I've included a huge list of words so you should still have plenty!

Question: Should students be given the entire list of words to study before the bee?

Answer: This depends on your philosophy and preference. Some educators feel that it is most fair when all students are given the exact words to study in advance. It "levels the playing field."

Others believe that this method only rewards those who can memorize the best, rather than those who can actually spell the best. By not giving students the entire list, the bee will reward students who can think on their feet, who have large spelling vocabularies, and who have studied on their own.

My recommendation is to use the 100-word study list provided in the Toolbox. About 70 of these words are in the actual big list. This gives students a taste of what to expect in the bee. Encourage students to study difficult words on their own, as well as to follow other tips included in this eBook.

Question: When conducting the spelling bee, should I use the words in the order they appear in the list of words and sentences, or mix them up randomly?

Answer: I strongly encourage you to use them in the order the appear. That's because the words are, generally speaking, arranged from easiest to most difficult. It makes sense to have the easiest words at the beginning of the bee. As spellers are eliminated, the remaining spellers should be given tougher and tougher words.
For example, it wouldn't be good for a speller to given *boulevard* in the first round, misspell it and be eliminated, then for another speller to be given the word *under* in the sixth round and advance. (Please note that you may want to rearrange a few words a bit by since difficulty is always somewhat subjective and can vary by curriculum, etc.)

THE SPELLING BEE TOOLBOX™
Spelling Bee Words and Sentences

See instructions on page 6. To see all the words included in the list, please refer to the alphabetical listing on page 68.

1. more – I always ask for more milk.

2. rule – We must obey every rule on the bus.

3. spent – I just spent my last one-dollar bill.

4. son – Nancy's son is a policeman.

5. bread – My grandma bakes the best bread!

6. done – Mr. Smith is done mowing the grass.

7. point – I always use a pencil with a sharp point.

8. should – You should cover your mouth when you sneeze.

9. blind – The blind man walked with a white cane.

10. litter – Please put all your trash in the litter basket.

11. mail – Our mail is not delivered on Sundays.

12. rode – The motorcyclist rode his bike all day.

13. knew – I knew the answer to the question.

14. school – Math is my favorite subject in school.

15. balloon – The hot-air balloon was beautiful to watch.

16. hurt – I hurt my leg when I fell down the stairs.

17. dinner – We had shrimp and salad for dinner.

18. boxes – The moving van was full of heavy boxes.

19. there – There will be a special guest tomorrow at school.

20. offer – We made an offer to buy the used car.

21. meat – Grandpa likes to eat meat and potatoes every night.

22. your – What is your name?

23. law – A policeman's job is to enforce the law.

24. classes – Susan takes college classes at night.

25. lamb – A young sheep is called a *lamb*.

26. once – Once upon a time, there were three little pigs.

27. roll – Can you roll an egg across the floor?

28. someone – Someone should close the door.

29. bright – Please don't shine a bright light in my face!

30. warm – I like to be outside on a warm day.

31. runner – Each runner who finished the race received a medal.

32. June – June is the sixth month of the year.

33. clear – On a clear day, you can see across the lake.

34. newspaper – Gary reads the newspaper every night before dinner.

35. piece – I'd like one piece of pepperoni pizza.

36. I've – I've always wanted to visit London.

37. dollar – We love to shop at the store where everything costs one dollar.

38. cheese – Tommy sprinkled a lot of cheese on his spaghetti.

39. children – Sometimes young children are afraid of the dark.

40. sky – Can you see the airplane up in the sky?

41. that's – That's the funniest joke I've ever heard!

42. sitting – The dog was sitting in the sun, warming himself.

43. why – Why is the rain so noisy?

44. soft – The kitten's fur is very soft.

45. windy – March is often a very windy month.

46. almost – The horse almost got away from its owner.

47. knee – The baseball player injured his knee.

48. merry – May all your Christmases be merry and filled with joy!

49. stale – The cookies taste stale because they are very old.

50. always – We always brush our teeth before we go to bed.

51. early – I get up early on school days.

52. none – None of us knew the secret password.

53. seventh – My father was the seventh child in his family.

54. serve – The waiter will serve the dessert last.

55. quickly – Please take your seats quickly before the bell rings.

56. slept – The police chief had not slept for two days.

57. caught – My dad caught a very bad cold from someone at work.

58. sew – My aunt likes to sew her own clothes.

59. writing – The author is writing a new book about parakeets.

60. under – When it's raining, I like to stand under an umbrella.

61. sunny – Since it's so warm and sunny outside, let's go to the beach.

62. flies – My new kite flies really well.

63. coming – When will Aunt Ann be coming for dinner?

64. summer – Last summer we drove to the ocean.

65. won't – The store won't be open until 10 A.M.

66. suitcase – I am allowed to take only one suitcase on the airplane.

67. match – Mom asked me to match up all of our odd socks.

68. spread – Harry likes to spread a lot of peanut butter on his toast.

69. marches – The high school band marches in perfect step.

70. biggest – This year's fair is the biggest one yet.

71. very – I am very excited to be here today!

72. lively – They played lively music at the square dance.

73. said – The teacher said we should work quietly.

74. agree – Bob and Joe agree on their favorite football teams.

75. zero – The losing team scored zero points during the game.

76. laugh – Clowns always make me laugh.

77. forgotten – The dog barked because I'd forgotten to feed him.

78. I'll – I'll be home as soon as the baseball game is finished.

79. heard – Have you heard about the big snowstorm?

80. build – I like to build interesting shapes with blocks.

81. every – Every person has a special talent.

82. between – I found an old leaf between the pages of a book.

83. junk – To me, some things sold at yard sales look like junk.

84. sore – His muscles were sore from lifting heavy bricks all day.

85. weren't – We weren't trying to make you late to the party.

86. aboard – The captain asked all passengers to climb aboard the ship.

87. calf – The newborn calf stayed close to its mother.

88. know – We know the best route to the coast.

89. happen – What will happen after we open the door?

90. movie – I really like the newest Disney movie.

91. only – Shelly is the only one who knows the answer.

92. people – Lots of people are expected to attend the concert.

93. before – Be sure to wash your hands before dinner.

94. other – The dog ran the other way.

95. half – Would you like the other half of my apple?

96. front – Please write your name on the front of your paper.

97. friend – My best friend is moving to California.

98. mouth – The dentist asked me to open my mouth.

99. wrote – Sally wrote a letter to her cousin.

100. tries – Dad always tries to make me laugh in the car

101. fences – We built new fences around the doghouse.

102. twelve - There are twelve eggs in a dozen.

103. path – The path took us through the woods.

104. trouble – Henry continues to have trouble with his sore knee.

105. Friday – My favorite day of the week is Friday.

106. own – My brother says he wants to own a mansion someday.

107. carries – Jack carries ten bricks at one time.

108. everyone – Everyone knows how much I like pretzels!

109. another – Let's find another route to the zoo.

110. worn – Randy's jeans are worn out.

111. again – I'd like to read that book again.

112. closest – You are sitting closest to the window.

113. until – Don't stop until you've finished the whole course.

114. says – Dad says I should always do my best.

115. afraid – The neighborhood kids were all afraid of Mr. Gibson's big dog.

116. because – Sam went to the store because he was out of milk.

117. maybe – Mom says maybe we can visit the zoo tomorrow.

118. cannot – My little sister cannot reach the top of the table.

119. doesn't – Bob doesn't want to go swimming.

120. young – My little sister is too young to ride a roller coaster.

121. heart – We put a big red heart on the door for Valentine's Day.

122. brushes - The hair salon cleans dozens of brushes every day.

123. picnic – Let's go to the park for a picnic.

124. heavy – I can't lift this rock because it's too heavy.

125. Monday – Our school week begins on Monday.

126. picture – The artist painted a picture of the flowers.

127. area – You'll find a lot of ski slopes in this area.

128. soggy – My cornflakes were soggy after sitting in milk for half an hour.

129. shelves – These shelves hold over 3,000 books.

130. tenth – The tenth letter of the alphabet is J.

131. morning – Our rooster crows every morning.

132. Thursday – Our class has music every Thursday.

133. across – The bridge is the best way to go across the river.

134. Saturday – We eat waffles for breakfast every Saturday.

135. foil – Mom covered the leftover food with foil.

136. shiny – The shiny coin sparkled on the cement.

137. whole – He ate the whole pizza by himself.

138. used – We like to shop for used furniture.

139. Tuesday – Tuesday marks the beginning of spring.

140. cents – One dime is worth ten cents.

141. everything – Everything in the store was on sale.

142. you're – You're the only person in the world who is just like you!

143. wiggle – It's fun to wiggle my loose tooth.

144. really – The soup is really hot!

145. streak – Please don't leave a streak on the window when you wash it.

146. grinned – He grinned from ear to ear when he opened the gift.

147. something – We want to do something special this weekend.

148. himself – If my baby brother reaches the scissors, he could hurt himself.

149. guess – It's hard to guess what tomorrow's weather will be.

150. collect – Bryce began to collect old pennies when he was five years old.

151. eyes – My eyes are red from cutting the onions.

152. straight – The worker arranged the cans in a straight row.

153. eleven – Eleven is one less than a dozen.

154. climb – The cat can climb a tree very quickly.

155. often – How often do you visit the ocean?

156. anywhere – Have you seen my glasses anywhere?

157. terrible – The rotten potatoes smell terrible!

158. thirteen – There are thirteen doughnuts in a baker's dozen.

159. second – The runner finished in second place.

160. active – The sick puppy was not very active.

161. breakfast – It's best to eat a good breakfast every morning.

162. eight – Four plus four equals eight.

163. believe – I believe it is best to always tell the truth.

164. style – My mom always wears the latest style of shoes.

165. guard – The bank hired a nighttime security guard.

166. fourteen – Two times seven is fourteen.

167. voice – Your voice is easy to recognize on the phone.

168. actor – Ben hopes to be a famous actor someday.

169. fifteen – The directions said to bake the muffins for fifteen minutes.

170. lonely – The college student felt lonely the first time she moved away from home.

171. stretch – It feels good to stretch in the morning.

172. together – Let's ride together to the store.

173. dear – My neighbor is a dear, elderly woman.

174. answer – If you know the answer, please raise your hand.

175. crumble – This cookie will crumble when you try to eat it.

176. mistake – My first mistake was not reading the directions.

177. doctor – I went to the doctor when I was ill.

178. busy – Uncle Joe keeps very busy with his work.

179. cities – We visited the cities of Dallas and Fort Worth.

180. stapler – You'll need to fill the stapler before you finish assembling the reports.

181. aunt – My aunt is visiting us from Canada.

182. written – Your report must be written in ink.

183. beggar – The beggar was cold and hungry.

184. healthy – The new parents were thankful for their healthy baby.

185. library – I go to the library once a week.

186. useful – A can opener is a very useful gadget.

187. January – We often get snow in January.

188. except – My little brother likes all vegetables except spinach.

189. sixty – Sixty is the sum of twenty and forty.

190. nickel – A nickel is worth five cents.

191. earth – The earth revolves around the sun once a year.

192. mirror – I looked in the mirror to check my hair.

193. soften – The recipe says to soften the bread crumbs in milk.

194. usually – We usually go to my grandma's house on Sunday.

195. squirt – The leaky hose will squirt water until it is repaired.

196. imagine – Let's imagine a beautiful day at the beach.

197. honor – The dinner was held in honor of her birthday.

198. seventy – My grandfather will be seventy years old next month.

199. wherever – Wherever you go on vacation, I'm sure you'll have a great time.

200. interested – Sheila is interested in taking computer classes.

201. can't – I can't find my glasses.

202. quiet – It's always quiet at the library.

203. chose – He chose the blue shirt, not the brown shirt.

204. crayon – I like to color with a sharpened crayon.

205. easier – It's easier to pull weeds in damp soil than in dry soil.

206. carrying – Are you carrying a heavy backpack?

207. juice – Orange juice is my favorite breakfast drink.

208. electric – We use an electric pencil sharpener.

209. studying – Tomorrow we'll be studying new spelling words.

210. knight – The knight rode a black horse into the forest.

211. drawer – My jeans are in the bottom drawer of my dresser.

212. forty – We need forty cups and plates for the party.

213. touch – Be careful not to touch the flat screen monitor with your fingers.

214. gazing – My dad sat quietly, gazing in the distance.

215. builder – Every builder in town buys his supplies at my dad's hardware.

216. beautiful – It's a beautiful day for a picnic.

217. fifty – Two quarters are worth fifty cents.

218. chimneys – Several chimneys in the old neighborhood were starting to crumble.

219. camera – Dad takes good pictures with his digital camera.

220. wrist – Sonya sprained her wrist doing a cartwheel.

221. December – December is the last month of the year.

222. allowance – Jake receives five dollars every week for an allowance.

223. hour – We waited for one hour at the doctor's office.

224. damage – The windstorm caused widespread damage.

225. husband – Paula's husband works at a bank.

226. angel – Sara played the part of an angel in the Christmas play.

227. October – Halloween is in October.

228. metal – The jewelry was made from a special type of metal.

229. equals – Three plus five equals eight.

230. nineteen – Twenty people were invited to the party, but only nineteen came.

231. rough – The road was very rough because of its many potholes.

232. fountain – Water from the drinking fountain is cold and refreshing.

233. companies – Three companies donated toys to needy children.

234. neighbor – My neighbor bakes the best cookies!

235. August – Our school year begins in August.

236. keys – The car dealer gave the keys to the new owner.

237. quite – I'm quite sure I put my book on the table.

238. rising – Fewer people traveled on vacation because of rising gas prices.

239. earliest – The earliest I can be at your house is 8 P.M.

240. September – We rake a lot of leaves in September.

241. nervous – My cat gets nervous in thunderstorms.

242. thirty – Ten plus twenty is thirty.

243. famous – A famous actress visited our restaurant.

244. remember – Alice could not remember where she put her purse.

245. February – Valentine's Day is in February.

246. surprise – It's fun to plan a surprise party for a friend.

247. Wednesday – Mom always shops on Wednesday.

248. twenty – Twenty students in our class signed up to go on the trip.

249. hungry – I'm so hungry, I could eat a horse!

250. double – I ordered a double scoop of chocolate ice cream.

251. tomorrow – The teacher asked us to do the homework by tomorrow.

252. grocery – I like to shop at the grocery store down the street.

253. important – Don't miss this important message.

254. November – We celebrate Thanksgiving in November.

255. handsome – Mom always tells my brother that he's very handsome.

256. families – Several families held yard sales together.

257. shouldn't – It shouldn't be a problem to get to school on time.

258. sixth – My aunt teaches sixth grade.

259. bought – We bought a new table at the furniture store.

260. hospital – Joe went to the hospital to visit his grandmother.

261. feather – A feather can tickle your skin.

262. happiest – Her wedding day was the happiest day of her life.

263. engine – The engine on the old truck was hard to start in winter.

264. calves – Three of the cows had calves at the same time.

265. choice – Making the right choice isn't always easy.

266. monkeys – Five monkeys climbed the ladders in their cage at the zoo.

267. ninth – The baseball game was tied in the ninth inning.

268. howl – Have you ever heard a coyote howl at night?

269. kitchen – The kitchen is the friendliest room in the house.

270. movement – I saw the movement of our dog out of the corner of my eye.

271. eighty – Forty plus forty is eighty.

272. knock – Since the doorbell is broken, you'll need to knock on the door.

273. grown – Grandma says I have grown a lot since the last time she saw me.

274. fourth – We had to leave the football game in the fourth quarter.

275. sneeze – Spicy foods make me sneeze.

276. either – Either Jim or Jane will need to make a phone call

277. fifth – My favorite chapter in this book is the fifth one.

278. rewind – We used to rewind VCR movies after watching them.

279. laughter – You could hear the guests' laughter all the way down the street.

280. shoulder – He pushed up against the closed door with his shoulder.

281. continue – Let's continue this discussion after lunch.

282. pudding – Chocolate pudding is my favorite.

283. allow – Mr. James will not allow his students to chew gum in class.

284. knead – The baker will knead the bread dough before putting it in the pan.

285. pioneer – Some pioneer families traveled in covered wagons.

286. tropical – There are many palm trees on the tropical island.

287. yesterday – I finished my homework from yesterday.

288. tread – The tread on the old tires has worn smooth.

289. drought – The creek dried up because of the drought.

290. avenue – The street on which I live is called an avenue.

291. bandage – The nurse wrapped a bandage on his wound.

292. cardboard – My gift came inside a large cardboard box.

293. disappear – A lot of food will disappear if my big brother is really hungry!

294. worried – Mom was worried when her friend did not answer the phone.

295. lying – The jury believed the witness was lying.

296. pennies – She saved 85 pennies in her piggy bank.

297. apartment – Ben rented a new three-bedroom apartment in downtown New York.

298. sandwich – My favorite kind of sandwich is peanut butter and jelly.

299. footage – The news program showed footage from the scene of a tragic fire.

300. skeleton – We saw a gigantic dinosaur skeleton at the museum.

301. suddenly – The wind suddenly blew down the old barn.

302. cottage – Our family has a summer cottage on the lake.

303. whistle – I love the sound of a distant train whistle.

304. quarter – I have three nickels and one quarter in my pocket.

305. scariest – That was the scariest movie I've ever seen!

306. urge – Few people can resist the urge to taste a freshly–baked cinnamon roll.

307. peaceful – We enjoyed a peaceful day alone at the beach.

308. sauce – Grandma's spaghetti sauce is everyone's favorite.

309. striped – Our striped cat thinks she's a big tiger.

310. warn – The weather forecaster tried to warn folks about the blizzard.

311. decorate – Dan and Tina plan to decorate the baby's room.

312. question – If you don't understand my explanation, please ask me a question.

313. cymbal – The drummer hit the cymbal with a loud crash at the end of the song.

314. county – The courthouse is in the center of our county.

315. payment – Jan always makes her house payment on time.

316. object – Find an object in the room that is green and blue.

317. remove – Please remove your shoes before walking on the white carpeting.

318. explode – The unopened pop can might explode if you leave it in the freezer.

319. burying – Our dog has been burying bones all over the backyard.

320. captain – David was chosen captain of the football team.

321. toward – If you walk toward my cat very slowly, she won't run from you.

322. finally – I finally finished cleaning my room!

323. exactly – You found exactly the right answer to this difficult problem.

324. coffee – Mom likes coffee without caffeine.

325. valleys – The valleys are filled with green grass and fertile soil.

326. curtain – The curtain opened as the orchestra began to play.

327. photograph – We were glad to find a photograph of my great-great-grandfather.

328. reserve – Mona will reserve the banquet hall for the party.

329. careful – You can't be too careful when removing hot food from the oven.

330. women – The three women met for lunch.

331. enough – Mom says there is never enough time in a day.

332. noisy – It was very noisy at the championship game.

333. memorize – We should memorize the directions for making lemonade.

334. wrecked – Because the ship was wrecked in the storm, it sank in the ocean.

335. nothing – If you eat all the vegetables, there will be nothing left for your sister.

336. opposite – The opposite of *up* is *down.*

337. vowel – The vowel in the word *sink* is the letter i.

338. careless – By proofreading your paper, you can often catch careless mistakes.

339. board – The board used to build the bench was six feet long.

340. clothes – Mark's clothes were dirty because he played in the mud.

341. expect – We expect the package to arrive tomorrow.

342. favorite – My favorite subject has always been math.

343. fashion – Lisa always wears the latest fashion.

344. garbage – We take the garbage out every Monday night.

345. tighten – Be sure to tighten the lid on the milk before you put it away.

346. hopeful – I am hopeful that I will finish the big project tonight.

347. grounded – All flights were grounded due to the dense fog.

348. countries – Three countries joined together on a new trade agreement.

349. cricket – We heard the large cricket chirping at night.

350. split – The jury was split on whether or not to convict the man of the crime.

351. guest – I'd love to be the guest of the Queen.

352. bruise – I have a big bruise on my knee because I fell down the stairs.

353. effort – Make every effort to be prepared for emergencies.

354. received – We received the good news that we'd won a big prize.

355. friendliness– Our neighborhood is known for its friendliness to newcomers.

356. doubtful – I am doubtful that anyone will be out in this bad weather.

357. desert – The ride through the desert was long and hot.

358. dinosaur – We enjoyed seeing the dinosaur fossils in the museum.

359. promising – The weather looks promising for a picnic today.

360. convince – Sally tried to convince her mother to let her go to the dance.

361. symbol – The Statue of Liberty is one symbol of freedom.

362. government – Top government officials met to discuss the war.

363. celebration – The New Year's celebration was a lot of fun.

364. daughter – Sarah's daughter looks and acts exactly like Sarah.

365. paramount – It is of paramount importance that I speak to the principal at once.

366. syllable – Young kids usually learn to spell words of one syllable first.

367. dictionaries – You can check the meaning of a word in any of our dictionaries.

368. determine – Let's determine the best plan of action.

369. column – Please write the numbers from 1 to 10 in the left column.

370. vanilla – My favorite ice cream flavor is vanilla.

371. capitol – The state senators met in the capitol building.

372. wound – This wound may require stitches.

373. critical – The patient was listed in critical condition.

374. height – The height of the ceiling in the ballroom was 20 feet.

375. instrumental – Jack was instrumental in getting the new project approved.

376. delicious – This apple pie is delicious!

377. eighth – My brother is an eighth grader this year.

378. hoarse – We were hoarse after cheering at the football game.

379. vanish – Mom says the food always seems to vanish when Uncle Lee visits us.

380. division – Division is the opposite of multiplication.

381. alarm - My alarm clock goes off at seven o'clock each morning.

382. arrangement – The teacher made a new seating arrangement for her class.

383. handling – We paid extra for shipping and handling.

384. whose – Mom wondered whose books were left in the car.

385. leafy – The salad made of dark leafy vegetables was very nutritious.

386. beetle – A beetle was eating a cabbage leave in our garden.

387. attention – It's hard to pay attention in school when you are really sleepy.

388. guide – Use the guide words to help you look up words in the dictionary.

389. knuckle – This ring is stuck on my knuckle.

390. listen – You can hear the birds chirping if you listen carefully.

391. pickle – A big dill pickle was served with the sandwich.

392. length – The length of time between her visits to the doctor was six months.

393. rely – You can't always rely on the weather report.

394. cereal – My dad's favorite kind of cereal is corn flakes.

395. minus – Five minus two equals three.

396. meant – I meant to ask you yesterday about your new pet.

397. simply – Let's decorate very simply and use only balloons.

398. poisoning – Matt's illness was caused by lead poisoning.

399. control – The race car driver struggled to control his car on the track.

400. statement – The doctor signed a statement so I could be excused from school.

401. several – Several of our friends are coming over for dinner.

402. mayor – Our mayor is organizing volunteers to work in his office.

403. steamy – The bathroom was steamy after my long, hot shower.

404. recently – We recently bought a new sofa.

405. poem – I'd like to write a poem about the silly things that happen to me.

406. vane – The weather vane on top of the barn spun around in the high wind.

407. weekend – We're going to a basketball game this weekend.

408. practice – All the practice paid off when the team won the championship.

409. postage – The large envelope required extra postage.

410. regional – Brenda finished second in the regional spelling bee.

411. manufacture – This factory will manufacture a new car model next year.

412. similar – Your idea is very similar to mine.

413. pleasant – Aunt Teri's visit was a pleasant surprise.

414. against – There were six votes for the plan and three votes against it.

415. staircase – The old staircase was narrow and creaky.

416. ruin – Spilling bleach on your clothes will ruin them.

417. trapeze – We loved watching the trapeze act at the circus.

418. measurement – Liters are used for liquid measurement.

419. impossible – It's impossible to know what *could* have happened.

420. salad – The chef served fruit salad with oranges, kiwi and bananas.

421. material – The jeans were made from very heavy material.

422. suggestion – His suggestion to postpone the meeting was a good one.

423. science – I like to do experiments in science class.

424. television – We gave our old television to the homeless shelter.

425. syrup – We put real maple syrup on our pancakes.

426. rescues – At the end of the movie, the hero rescues the little girl.

427. weight – Trucks have to follow weight limits on most roads and highways.

428. triangles – A square can be divided into two triangles.

429. probably – We will probably stay up late on Friday night.

430. business – Mom's website business is going very well.

431. supplying – The bakery will be supplying the cake for the wedding.

432. different – Rosa plays in three different movies.

433. surroundings – It's best to do your homework in quiet surroundings.

434. polish – I helped Dad wax and polish his car.

435. sandal – When my sandal broke, I had to walk barefooted.

436. radios – We could hear three radios playing at one time on our street.

437. phase –The first phase of the building is almost finished.

438. schedule - The flight delay changed our entire vacation schedule.

439. pleasure – My neighbor finds much pleasure in her garden.

440. minor – It's best not to get too upset about minor problems.

441. scent – When a skunk feels scared, it gives off an unmistakable scent.

442. rarely – A kangaroo is rarely seen in my country.

443. although – Although we've never met before, I feel like I already know you.

444. inventor – Thomas Edison was an important inventor.

445. necessary – It is necessary that we go outside during a fire drill.

446. capital – Each sentence should begin with a capital letter.

447. unknown – An unknown person gave a large sum of money to our school.

448. vacation – I've always wanted to go to Florida for vacation.

449. amusement – The amusement park will be open all summer.

450. chemical – David received special training in handling chemical spills.

451. tasty – This vegetable pizza is very tasty!

452. chocolate – We like to drink hot chocolate in the winter.

453. protection – Hats, boots and gloves provide good protection from the cold.

454. amendment – Congress wants to pass a new amendment to our constitution.

455. happily – I will happily help you spread your good news!

456. messages – I left three messages on her answering machine.

457. paragraph – Each paragraph should contain one main idea.

458. stomach – I wonder if anyone heard my stomach growl.

459. separate – The fourth and fifth graders eat in separate lunchrooms.

460. ought – I ought to finish my chores before I watch television.

461. sweater – Sally was cold, so she put on a sweater.

462. numeral – The Roman numeral for 5 is a V.

463. tornado – The tornado damaged the high school and fire station.

464. straighten – Mr. Wilson asked us to straighten the row of chairs.

465. tissue – Be sure you have a tissue in your pocket when you have a cold.

466. swollen – The doctor could see that her tonsils were swollen.

467. earnest – I will try in earnest to complete this assignment on time.

468. source – A pinched nerve was the source of his back pain.

469. slippery – The sign said the road would be slippery when wet.

470. shadows – It's fun to make animal shapes with finger shadows.

471. wheelchair –Grandma uses a wheelchair because her legs are weak.

472. typewriter – The author likes to type his stories on a typewriter, not a computer.

473. carefully – Drive carefully on snow-covered roads.

474. consonant – The first consonant in the alphabet is the letter B.

475. occurs – The letter e occurs in words more often than any other letter in English.

476. vault – The bank keeps one million dollars of cash in its vault.

477. knowledge – When you read a lot of books, your knowledge is sure to increase.

478. inquire – Mom called customer service to inquire about the bill.

479. especially – I am especially fond of my cousins, Kyle and Kelsie.

480. patient – It's hard to be patient when something wonderful is about to happen.

481. sailor – The sailor had been away at sea for six months.

482. heroes – Fire fighters and police officers are everyday heroes.

483. reign – Queen Elizabeth has had a very long reign.

484. legal – It is not legal to drive at age 10.

485. manager – The store manager hired three new workers.

486. concern – My doctor showed great concern over my high fever.

487. edition – The afternoon edition of the paper included the latest news.

488. scarcely – There is scarcely enough water in the bathtub to wash your feet.

489. temperature – The temperature today is ten degrees lower than yesterday.

490. acquire – Some people try not to acquire very many possessions.

491. believable – She received a lot of votes because her message was so believable.

492. strengthen – These exercises will help to strengthen your legs.

493. champion – The champion steer won the grand prize at the fair.

494. emptiness – The emptiness of the open prairie surprised the city dwellers.

495. fossil – We found an interesting fossil on the beach.

496. honorable – For Donna, the honorable solution was to tell the truth.

497. educate – Ann likes to help educate people who move to her city as immigrants.

498. encyclopedia – Our encyclopedia set has ten volumes.

499. freight – One truck can carry several tons of freight.

500. hamburger – I like the taste of a grilled hamburger.

501. beautifully – The wedding dress turned out beautifully!

502. disagreement – Our disagreement has not hurt our friendship.

503. excitement – It's hard for Sam to control the excitement about his birthday.

504. forgiveness – Shelly asked for Tom's forgiveness for the unkind words she said.

505. forgetting – I keep forgetting where I put my keys.

506. concentration – Glassblowers must work with great concentration.

507. addresses – We need addresses for everyone we want to invite to the party.

508. altogether – Three of us spent $100 altogether at the electronics store.

509. cradle – Jack made a beautiful cradle for his newborn baby.

510. exploration – There has been limited exploration for oil in some regions.

511. creative – Emily makes creative gifts every year for her friends.

512. prevention - The crime prevention officer teaches classes on safety.

513. collapse – If we build this house of cards any taller, I'm sure it will collapse.

514. amphibian – A frog is an amphibian because it lives both in and out of water.

515. conclude – This meeting will conclude at 8 P.M.

516. automobile – The automobile is probably the most popular form of transportation.

517. invitation – We received an invitation to my cousin's graduation party.

518. assignment – The math assignment is due tomorrow.

519. confuse – It's easy to confuse words like *then* and *than.*

520. prairie – We saw hundreds of cattle grazing on the prairie.

521. potato – We planted six potato plants in our garden.

522. enormous – The blue whale is the most enormous mammal of all.

523. exchange – Mom went back to the store to exchange the sweater.

524. forecast – The weather forecast calls for sunshine tomorrow.

525. gracious – Eve is very gracious, even when she loses a game.

526. insert – You must insert only quarters in this vending machine.

527. predict – It's hard to predict which team will win this game.

528. instance – This is one instance where we should stay inside.

529. absence – You'll need a doctor's note to be excused for your absence.

530. condition – The antique books were still in excellent condition.

531. anchor – The captain dropped the ship's anchor during the storm.

532. artistic – The sculpture was a fine example of artistic expression.

533. gesture – Please accept this gesture of good will from our country to yours.

534. decimal – We learned how to change fractions to decimal numbers.

535. lawyer – Betsy is in law school, studying to become a lawyer.

536. pumpkins – We carve big pumpkins each year at Halloween.

537. penguin – The penguin family waddled into the water.

538. performance – The violinist gave his best performance ever.

539. wrestle – Jim continues to wrestle with the decision of changing jobs.

540. strategy – I learned a great strategy for winning at checkers.

541. wolves – Wolves are the largest members of the dog family.

542. tomatoes – Mary grows her own tomatoes and uses them to make salsa.

543. acquainted – I want to get acquainted with our new neighbors.

544. recommend – The teacher likes to recommend good books.

545. twentieth – This is the twentieth year of Rob and Amy's business partnership.

546. system – The accountant used a new system to record income and expenses.

547. unite – We all need to unite and support our new president.

548. trivial – There is no point in getting upset about trivial matters.

549. naughty – Most young children know when they've been naughty.

550. irritate – Wearing scratchy fabrics can irritate your skin.

551. complication – Because of the legal complication, her court case was thrown out.

552. adorable – The new kitten was simply adorable!

553. courage – It sometimes requires courage to do the right thing.

554. pertinent – The judge asked the witness to tell only the most pertinent facts.

555. spectacles – Gramps lost his spectacles when they fell off the end of his nose.

556. intermission – We'll buy more popcorn at intermission.

557. prompt – Keith is prompt for every appointment.

558. fantastic – The most fantastic thing happened when pigs fell from the sky!

559. moderator – The moderator for the political debate was fair and objective.

560. competitive – Jake's secret to success was keeping his prices competitive.

561. toxic – Fumes from the burning chemicals were toxic, so no one went outside.

562. proficiency – A plumber must pass a proficiency exam before receiving a license.

563. immediately – When the smoke detector sounded, we immediately left the house.

564. independence – The United States fought for independence from Great Britain.

565. obstacle – The only obstacle to her success as a doctor was her fear of blood.

566. exhibit – The art exhibit featured paintings from French artists.

567. astronaut – Danny wants to be an astronaut and fly to the moon.

568. extinct – The dodo bird has been extinct for a long time.

569. atmosphere – Our atmosphere contains oxygen and carbon dioxide.

570. algae – The algae washed up on shore, covering the shells and sand.

571. character – My favorite character in the cartoon was a chipmunk.

572. cashier – The cashier at the convenience store was very friendly.

573. deceive – The would-be thief tried to deceive the bank teller.

574. interrupt – It's not polite to interrupt someone when they are talking.

575. luxury – The millionaire's luxury items include a yacht and a home in Paris.

576. lightning – The tree was split in two when it was struck by lightning.

577. restaurant – Our family likes to eat at this Chinese restaurant.

578. scholar – The scholar spends much of his time doing reading and research.

579. stationary – A two-ton boulder is a stationary object.

580. symphony – My favorite symphony was composed by Bach.

581. theater – We saw a movie at the theater last weekend.

582. thorough – After a thorough search of the car, we still could not find the map.

583. extinguish – Firefighters worked through the night to extinguish the flames.

584. tournament – Thirty-two teams were scheduled to play in the tournament.

585. unnecessary – It's unnecessary to apologize for your hiccups.

586. sheriff – The county sheriff hired two new deputies.

587. whirlpool – Mr. Johnson gets relief from his arthritis by taking whirlpool baths.

588. brochure – We read a colorful brochure about Australia.

589. boundary – It is unclear where the boundary lies because the fence is gone.

590. accompanied – Each child under 12 must be accompanied by an adult.

591. unfortunately – Unfortunately, we were unable to go to the airport with my dad.

592. chauffeur – Mrs. Smith's chauffeur drives her to the hair salon every Friday.

593. guacamole – We ordered guacamole with chips as an appetizer.

594. precipitation – Sleet and snow are two forms of precipitation.

595. triennial – A triennial conference is held once every three years.

596. embarrass – I won't embarrass Beth by calling her by her real name.

597. jaguar – The jaguar was on the prowl, looking for something to eat.

598. commitment – Stan's boss was impressed by Stan's commitment to his job.

599. sulfur – The sulfur was used to make kitchen matches.

600. controlling – The kicker was having a hard time controlling the ball in the wind.

601. distinguished – After years of distinguished service, the lieutenant retired.

602. questionnaire – Please fill out this questionnaire about your favorite foods.

603. boulevard – The city planted new trees along our boulevard.

604. badminton – Paul was unable to play badminton because he lost his racket.

605. malnutrition – The poor children were ill due to hunger and malnutrition.

606. rhythm – The drummer played a strong rhythm for the band's new song.

607. acquisition – The firm decided to expand after its acquisition of additional space.

608. meringue – Lemon meringue pie is a specialty at Faith's bakery.

609. misdemeanor – Ted received only a fine since his crime was a misdemeanor.

610. paralysis – After the stroke, Henry's legs suffered from paralysis.

611. threatening – The threatening sky meant the storm was about to start.

612. opossum – We saw an opossum family scurry across the road.

613. reservoir – There's a large reservoir at the site of the dam.

614. typhoon – The island was completely flooded in the typhoon.

615. afghan – Esther knitted an afghan for each of her grandchildren.

616. chronology – Mitch recited an accurate chronology of the events of World War II.

617. rhinoceros – We're hoping to see a rhinoceros when we go on safari.

618. cologne – This smells like a very expensive cologne.

619. pneumonia – The patient had a difficult time recovering from pneumonia.

620. zucchini – We like to eat zucchini grilled with onions.

THE SPELLING BEE TOOLBOX™
Alphabetical Listing of Our 620 Spelling Bee Words

1. aboard	40. attention	79. can't
2. absence	41. August	80. capital
3. accompanied	42. aunt	81. capitol
4. acquainted	43. automobile	82. captain
5. acquire	44. avenue	83. cardboard
6. acquisition	45. badminton	84. careful
7. across	46. balloon	85. carefully
8. active	47. bandage	86. careless
9. actor	48. beautiful	87. carries
10. addresses	49. beautifully	88. carrying
11. adorable	50. because	89. cashier
12. afghan	51. beetle	90. caught
13. afraid	52. before	91. celebration
14. again	53. beggar	92. cents
15. against	54. believable	93. cereal
16. agree	55. believe	94. champion
17. algae	56. between	95. character
18. alarm	57. biggest	96. chauffeur
19. allow	58. blind	97. cheese
20. allowance	59. board	98. chemical
21. almost	60. bought	99. children
22. although	61. boulevard	100. chimneys
23. altogether	62. boundary	101. chocolate
24. always	63. boxes	102. choice
25. amendment	64. bread	103. chose
26. amphibian	65. breakfast	104. chronology
27. amusement	66. bright	105. cities
28. anchor	67. brochure	106. classes
29. angel	68. bruise	107. clear
30. another	69. brushes	108. climb
31. answer	70. build	109. closest
32. anywhere	71. builder	110. clothes
33. apartment	72. burying	111. coffee
34. area	73. business	112. collapse
35. arrangement	74. busy	113. collect
36. artistic	75. calf	114. cologne
37. assignment	76. calves	115. column
38. astronaut	77. camera	116. coming
39. atmosphere	78. cannot	117. commitment

118. companies
119. competitive
120. complication
121. concentration
122. concern
123. conclude
124. condition
125. confuse
126. consonant
127. continue
128. control
129. controlling
130. convince
131. cottage
132. countries
133. county
134. courage
135. cradle
136. crayon
137. creative
138. cricket
139. critical
140. crumble
141. curtain
142. cymbal
143. damage
144. daughter
145. dear
146. deceive
147. December
148. decimal
149. decorate
150. delicious
151. desert
152. determine
153. dictionaries
154. different
155. dinner
156. dinosaur
157. disagreement
158. disappear
159. distinguished

160. division
161. doctor
162. doesn't
163. dollar
164. done
165. double
166. doubtful
167. drawer
168. drought
169. earliest
170. early
171. earnest
172. earth
173. easier
174. edition
175. educate
176. effort
177. eight
178. eighth
179. eighty
180. either
181. electric
182. eleven
183. embarrass
184. emptiness
185. encyclopedia
186. engine
187. enormous
188. enough
189. equals
190. especially
191. every
192. everyone
193. everything
194. exactly
195. except
196. exchange
197. excitement
198. exhibit
199. expect
200. explode
201. exploration

202. extinct
203. extinguish
204. eyes
205. families
206. famous
207. fantastic
208. fashion
209. favorite
210. feather
211. February
212. fences
213. fifteen
214. fifth
215. fifty
216. finally
217. flies
218. foil
219. footage
220. forecast
221. forgetting
222. forgiveness
223. forgotten
224. forty
225. fossil
226. fourteen
227. fourth
228. fountain
229. freight
230. Friday
231. friend
232. front
233. friendliness
234. garbage
235. gazing
236. gesture
237. government
238. gracious
239. grinned
240. grocery
241. grounded
242. grown
243. guacamole

244. guard
245. guess
246. guest
247. guide
248. half
249. hamburger
250. handling
251. handsome
252. happen
253. happiest
254. happily
255. healthy
256. heard
257. heart
258. heavy
259. height
260. heroes
261. himself
262. hoarse
263. honor
264. honorable
265. hopeful
266. hospital
267. hour
268. howl
269. hungry
270. hurt
271. husband
272. I'll
273. I've
274. imagine
275. immediately
276. important
277. impossible
278. independence
279. inquire
280. insert
281. instance
282. instrumental
283. interested
284. intermission
285. interrupt

286. inventor
287. invitation
288. irritate
289. jaguar
290. January
291. juice
292. June
293. junk
294. keys
295. kitchen
296. knead
297. knee
298. knew
299. knight
300. knock
301. know
302. knowledge
303. knuckle
304. lamb
305. laugh
306. laughter
307. law
308. lawyer
309. leafy
310. legal
311. length
312. library
313. lightning
314. listen
315. litter
316. lively
317. lonely
318. luxury
319. lying
320. mail
321. malnutrition
322. manager
323. manufacture
324. marches
325. match
326. material
327. maybe

328. mayor
329. meant
330. measurement
331. meat
332. memorize
333. meringue
334. merry
335. messages
336. metal
337. minor
338. minus
339. mirror
340. misdemeanor
341. mistake
342. moderator
343. Monday
344. monkeys
345. more
346. morning
347. mouth
348. movie
349. movement
350. naughty
351. necessary
352. neighbor
353. nervous
354. newspaper
355. nickel
356. nineteen
357. ninth
358. noisy
359. none
360. nothing
361. November
362. numeral
363. object
364. obstacle
365. occur
366. October
367. offer
368. often
369. once

370. only
371. opossum
372. opposite
373. other
374. ought
375. own
376. paragraph
377. paralysis
378. paramount
379. path
380. patient
381. payment
382. peaceful
383. penguin
384. pennies
385. people
386. performance
387. pertinent
388. photograph
389. phase
390. pickle
391. picnic
392. picture
393. piece
394. pioneer
395. pleasant
396. pleasure
397. pneumonia
398. poem
399. point
400. poisoning
401. polish
402. potato
403. postage
404. practice
405. prairie
406. precipitation
407. predict
408. prevention
409. probably
410. proficiency
411. promising
412. prompt

413. protection
414. pudding
415. pumpkins
416. quarter
417. question
418. questionnaire
419. quickly
420. quiet
421. quite
422. radios
423. rarely
424. really
425. received
426. recently
427. recommend
428. regional
429. reign
430. rely
431. remember
432. remove
433. rescues
434. reserve
435. reservoir
436. restaurant
437. rewind
438. rhinoceros
439. rhythm
440. rising
441. rode
442. roll
443. rough
444. ruin
445. rule
446. runner
447. said
448. sailor
449. salad
450. sandal
451. sandwich
452. Saturday
453. sauce
454. says
455. scarcely

456. scariest
457. scent
458. schedule
459. scholar
460. school
461. science
462. second
463. separate
464. September
465. serve
466. seventh
467. seventy
468. several
469. sew
470. shadows
471. shelves
472. sheriff
473. shiny
474. should
475. shoulder
476. shouldn't
477. similar
478. simply
479. sitting
480. sixth
481. sixty
482. skeleton
483. sky
484. slept
485. slippery
486. sneeze
487. soft
488. soften
489. soggy
490. someone
491. something
492. son
493. sore
494. source
495. spectacles
496. spent
497. split
498. spread

499. squirt	540. thirteen	581. vane
500. staircase	541. thirty	582. vanilla
501. stale	542. thorough	583. vanish
502. stapler	543. threatening	584. vault
503. statement	544. Thursday	585. very
504. stationary	545. tighten	586. voice
505. steamy	546. tissue	587. vowel
506. stomach	547. together	588. warm
507. straight	548. tomatoes	589. warn
508. straighten	549. tomorrow	590. Wednesday
509. strategy	550. tornado	591. weekend
510. streak	551. touch	592. weight
511. strengthen	552. tournament	593. weren't
512. stretch	553. toward	594. wheelchair
513. striped	554. toxic	595. wherever
514. studying	555. trapeze	596. whirlpool
515. style	556. tread	597. whistle
516. suddenly	557. triangles	598. whole
517. suggestion	558. triennial	599. whose
518. suitcase	559. tries	600. why
519. sulfur	560. trivial	601. wiggle
520. summer	561. tropical	602. windy
521. sunny	562. trouble	603. wolves
522. supplying	563. Tuesday	604. women
523. surprise	564. twelve	605. won't
524. surroundings	565. twentieth	606. worn
525. sweater	566. twenty	607. worried
526. swollen	567. typhoon	608. wound
527. syllable	568. typewriter	609. wrecked
528. symbol	569. under	610. wrestle
529. symphony	570. unfortunately	611. wrist
530. syrup	571. unite	612. writing
531. system	572. unknown	613. written
532. tasty	573. unnecessary	614. wrote
533. television	574. until	615. yesterday
534. temperature	575. urge	616. you're
535. tenth	576. used	617. young
536. terrible	577. useful	618. your
537. that's	578. usually	619. zero
538. theater	579. vacation	620. zucchini
539. there	580. valleys	

THE SPELLING BEE TOOLBOX™
Super Challenge Words

If your spellers manage to breeze through all the words in our list above, use these 30 super-challenge words for your spelling bee. We've included the language of origin, **primary** pronunciation, and part of speech, the most common definition and one sentence for each word. ***Please note that every effort has been made to ensure the accuracy of all information for each word. Occasionally, sources differ on some items.***

Pronunciations

We've included the most popular pronunciations. Additional pronunciations may exist for some words. We've chosen to use very few special symbols and markings.

Pronunciation Guide:

(a) - as in *sad, tap, latch*
(ā) - as in *a* in *pay, late, cape*
(ä) - as in *father, hot*
(e) - as in *led, set, deck*
(ē) - as in *feel, deal, easy*
(ə) - as in **a**bout, **c**onfuse

(i) - as in *lip, fish*
(ī) - as in *tide, white, ripe*
(ō) - as in *cone, rope, snow*
(u) - as in *sun, umbrella*
(oo) - as in *poodle*
(yoo) - as in *bugle, uniform*

(g) – as in **g**um, **g**orilla
(t) - any letter inside parenthesis within another syllable may or may not be pronounced.

The main emphasis in each word belongs on the syllable in **bold** type.

Word List

1. plumage (**ploo**-mij) *Old French* noun: the feathers of a bird
    The peacock showed off its colorful plumage.

2. mozzarella (mot-sə-**rel**-lə) *Italian* noun: a white, soft cheese
    We asked for extra mozzarella on our pizza.

3. wrangle (**rang**-gəl) *Middle English* verb: to persistently argue, often loudly
    The two men were known to wrangle for hours before coming to any agreement.

4. monotonous (mə-**not**-n-əs) *Greek* adjective: dull, boring, repetitive or limited to
                a narrow pitch range
    The speaker's voice was so monotonous that it was hard for us to stay awake.

5. poinsettia (poin-**set**-ē-ə, or poin-**set**-ə) *new Latin* noun: colorful plant, usually
with scarlet, pink or white blossoms
We gave Mom a large red poinsettia plant at Christmastime.

6. quiche (kēsh) *French* noun: an unsweetened pie or pastry
The restaurant's most popular dish is spinach quiche.

7. exuberant (ig-**zoo**-ber-ənt) *Middle English* adjective: extremely enthusiastic
David was exuberant as he announced the birth of his son.

8. tarantula (tə-**ran**-chə-lə) *Latin, Italian* noun: one in a family of large hairy spiders
Even though the tarantula was safely contained in a cage, it still looked
frightening.

9. quesadilla (kā-sə-**dē**-ə) *Spanish* noun: a tortilla with cheese and other
ingredients, usually fried or grilled
My aunt served me a chicken quesadilla with salsa.

10. terrestrial (tə-**res**-trē-əl) *Latin* adjective: related to the earth
The science fiction movie contained all sorts of terrestrial creatures I could never
imagine!

11. clique (klēk or klik) *French*   noun: an exclusive group of people
Anna did not feel welcome in the clique of ninth grade girls.

12. fraudulent (fraw-jə-lənt) *Latin* adjective: deceptive or false
The insurance agent knew the man's claim was fraudulent.

13. oscillate (**os**-ə-lāt) *Latin* verb: to move back and forth
Please set the fan to oscillate so that everyone in the room will feel the breeze.

14. sassafras (**sas**-ə-fras) *Spanish* noun: a North American tree
As we walked past the line of sassafras, we could smell the fragrant bark.

15. pterodactyl (ter-ə-**dak**-til) *New Latin, Greek* noun: one of several extinct,
flying reptiles
The museum exhibit showed a pterodactyl flying above a brontosaurus.

16. salmonella (sal-mə-**nel**-ə) *New Latin* noun: a kind of bacteria that can
cause food poisoning
The sickness was traced to a restaurant whose eggs contained salmonella.

17. pachyderm (**pa**-ki-derm) *French and Greek* noun: a large mammal with a thick skin, especially the elephant, rhinoceros, or hippopotamus
The zookeeper needed special training to handle a pachyderm.

18. sumptuous (**səmp**-choo-əs) *Latin* adjective: splendid, extravagant or luxurious
Our tour of the magnificent castle ended with a sumptuous feast.

19. scalpel (**skal**-pəl) *Latin* noun: a small, sharp knife use in surgical procedures
When the surgeon was ready to begin, she asked for a scalpel.

20. mahogany (mə-**hog**-ə-nē) *Exact origin unknown* noun: a tropical hardwood tree or the reddish brown wood from the tree
The antique bookcase was made from mahogany.

21. ogre (**ō**-ger) *French* noun: a hideous monster in fairy tales and legends
Little Sammy screamed when the ugly ogre appeared on the movie screen.

22. luau (**loo**-ou) *Hawaiian* noun: a feast of Hawaiian food, usually held outdoors
The tourists looked forward to the food and dancing at the luau on their last night of vacation.

23. applique (ap-li-**kā**) *French* noun: a cutout design that is sewn onto a larger piece of material
Grandma made a quilt with applique flowers on green and white blocks.

24. pavilion (pə-**vil**-yən] *Middle English, Old French, Latin* noun: an open building used for shelter, exhibits or recreation
The Smiths held their family reunion at the pavilion in the city park.

25. obnoxious (əb-**nok**-shəs) *Latin* adjective: annoying, objectionable, or disliked
Many people thought the child was spoiled, demanding and very obnoxious.

26. masquerade (mas-kə-**rād**) *Spanish* noun: a party or dance at which people wear masks and disguises
We were told that many celebrities attended the masquerade, but we weren't sure who they were.

27. onyx (**on**-iks) *Middle English, Latin, Greek* noun: a variety of agate with colored layers
Laura ordered glossy black onyx worktops for her new kitchen cabinets.

28. toboggan (tə-**bog**-ən) *Canadian French* noun: a flat-bottomed wooden frame used
     for sliding over snow and ice
     The children loved riding the toboggan down the long slope of fresh snow.

29. ophthalmology (of-thəl-**mol**-ə-jee) *Greek* noun: the branch of medicine dealing
     with the eye and its diseases
     Robert has always been interested in the eye, so he will study ophthalmology in
     medical school.

30. chateaux (sha-**tō**) *French* noun: a country house, castle or manor house
     We rented a French chateaux for a luxury vacation last summer.

*Please note that every effort has been made to ensure the accuracy of all information
for each word. Occasionally, sources differ on some items.*

✼   ✼   ✼   ✼   ✼   ✼   ✼

THE SPELLING BEE TOOLBOX ™
Clip art, Bookmarks, Reminders, Name Tags and Award Certificates

Use these images to dress up your Spelling Bee written communications. Pick a single image to use over and over as a theme, or use a variety of images.

Don't get stung.

v

Be ready for the bee!

Our Spelling Bee

is something to BUZZ about!

It's Time to Get Excited

About Our Spelling Bee!

THE SPELLING BEE TOOLBOX ™
Book marks

Dive right in and study these spelling words!

_____

_____

_____

_____

_____

_____

_____

_____

_____

_____

My Top

10

Words to Study This Week:

_____

_____

_____

_____

_____

_____

_____

_____

_____

_____

"Bee" Sure You're Ready for the Spelling Bee!

z z z

z z z

z z z

Date:

_____

Time:

_____

Place:

_____

Spelling Bee Reminder

Date: _____

Time: _____

Place: _____

Other important info: _____

_____

_____

Spelling Bee Reminder

Date:_____

Time: _____

Place: _____

Other important info: _____

_____

_____

Name Tags
See directions on page 8.

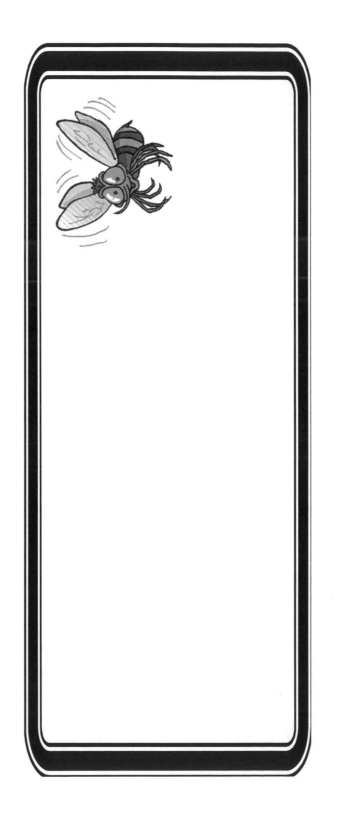

Spelling Excellence

This award goes to

_____

Winner of the

_____Spelling
Bee

held on _____, 20____

at

_____

Congratulations!

_____   _____
Principal   Teacher

Spelling Excellence

This award goes to

_____

_____- place finisher in the

_____Spelling Bee

held on _____, 20____

at

_____

Congratulations!

_____   _____
Principal   Teacher

© 2014 www.spelling–words-well.com

Spelling Excellence

In appreciation to

_____

for your participation in the

_____Spelling Bee

held on _____, 20_____

at

_____

Thank you!

_____   _____
Principal   Teacher

This award goes to

_____

Winner of the

_____Spelling Bee

held on _____, 20_____

at

_____

Your hard work has paid off.
Congratulations!

_____   _____
Principal   Teacher

This award goes to

_____

for finishing in ____ place

in the

_____ Spelling Bee

held on _____, 20____

at

_____

Great Work!

_____   _____
Principal   Teacher

This award goes to

_____

for your participation in the

_____ Spelling Bee

held on _____, 20_____

at

_____

Your participation and hard work
helped to make our spelling bee a success.
Thank you!

_____   _____
Principal   Teacher

Congratulations

to

_____

Winner

of the _____
Spelling Bee

Held on _____, 20_____

at

_____

Great Job!

_____   _____
Principal   Teacher

Congratulations

to

_____

for finishing in ____ place

in the _____

Spelling Bee

Held on _____, 20_____

at

_____

Great Job!

_____ _____
Principal   Teacher

This award goes to

_____

for your participation in the

_____

Spelling Bee

Held on _____, 20_____

at

_____

You helped to make our bee a success.
Thank You!

_____   _____
Principal   Teacher

This is to certify that

_____

was the

WINNER

of the

_____

Spelling Bee

held on _____, 20____

Congratulations!

_____   _____

This is to certify that

_____

finished in

_____ place

in the

_____

Spelling Bee

held on _____, 20___

Great Job!

_____   _____

This is to certify that

_____

participated in the

_____

Spelling Bee

held on _____, 20___

Thank you for helping to make our bee a success!

_____   _____

Congratulations
to

_____

Winner
of the

_____

Spelling Bee
_____, 20____

Signed _____
Title _____

Congratulations

to

_____

___- *Place Finisher*
in the

_____

Spelling Bee
_____, 20____

Signed _____
Title _____

This is to certify that

_____

participated
in the

_____

Spelling Bee
_____, 20____

Signed _____
Title _____

This Spelling Bee Certificate
is awarded to

_____

Winner

of the _____

Spelling Bee

on _____, 20 ____

at _____

Congratulations!

_____   _____
Spelling bee coordinator   Teacher

This Spelling Bee Certificate
is awarded to

_____

for finishing in

_____place

in the _____ Spelling Bee

held on _____, 20 ___

at _____

Congratulations!

_____   _____
Spelling Bee Coordinator   Teacher

This Spelling Bee Certificate

is awarded to

_____

for participating

in the _____ Spelling Bee

held on _____, 20 ___

at _____

Thank You!

_____   _____
Spelling Bee Coordinator   Teacher

For more full-color
Spelling Bee Certificates and Name Tags,

please go to:

http://www.spelling-words-well.com/support-files/colored-
certificates-gr3-5.pdf

The Spelling Bee Toolbox for Grades 3-5

NOTES

NOTES

_____

_____

_____

_____

_____

_____

_____

_____

_____

_____

_____

Thank you for purchasing the

THE SPELLING BEE TOOLBOX™
FOR GRADES 3-5

Also Available: *The Spelling Bee Toolbox for Grades 6-8*

Remember to visit www.spelling-words-well.com for more spelling ideas!
You'll find free worksheets, games, teaching tips, and activities.

You can also find us on Facebook.

About the Author
Ann Richmond Fisher, a former classroom and home school teacher, has been an educational freelance writer for over 25 years. Her innovative books, products and magazine articles have been published by several leading educational publishers. Contact her at spelling.words.well@gmail.com.

Ann is the owner of two websites:
      www.spelling-words-well.com
      www.word-game-world.com

Bryce may be contacted for his web design services through:
https://bryce.fisher-fleig.org/

Made in the USA
Lexington, KY
30 April 2017